Published by
Suzo Media

Book design by Chryss Yost
Cover art: Susan Read Cronin

© 2021 by Susan Read Cronin

All rights reserved
Printed in the United States of America

First edition

ISBN: 978-1-7350460-1-3

www.susanreadcronin.com

# OPEN

## Susan Read Cronin

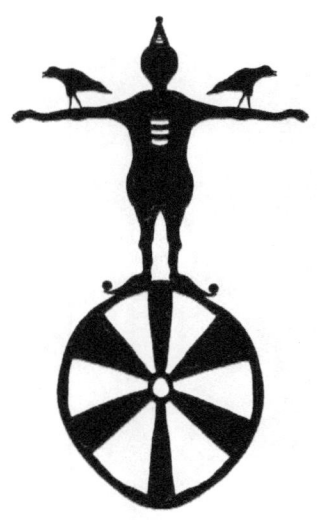

Suzo Media, Santa Barbara
2021

# TABLE OF CONTENTS

## EPISTLES TO GOD

| | |
|---|---|
| (Parentheses) | 15 |
| Second-Born Daughters | 16 |
| Womb with a View | 17 |
| Letting Go | 18 |
| When Our Parents Go Away, Willy Comes to Stay | 19 |
| The New Cook | 20 |
| Clamming | 21 |
| How to Be a Three-Year-Old | 23 |
| About Morons | 24 |
| Teacup Pareidolia | 25 |
| Hunting Up a Poem | 26 |
| Fritter the Day Away | 27 |
| Epistles to God | 28 |
| The Glimpse | 30 |
| You, Sleeping Beside Her | 31 |
| Accidents Happen | 32 |
| Quid Pro Crow | 33 |
| My Sister's Ring | 34 |
| The Altar | 35 |
| The Extraordinary Sex Life of the Slipper Limpet | 36 |

| | |
|---|---|
| At the Pier | 37 |
| Inside Out | 38 |
| Settling the Estate | 39 |

## I LOST MY BABY TEETH AND MY VIRGINITY IN A HOUSE EATEN BY TERMITES

| | |
|---|---|
| Why | 45 |
| Mondrian's Sock Drawer | 46 |
| Red | 47 |
| The Neighbors' Tommyrot | 49 |
| To the Wealthy Old Man Who Left His Wife of Fifty Years for a Much Younger Woman | 50 |
| Marriage Metaphors | 51 |
| Lying in the Confessional | 52 |
| Maybe You Know That Guy— | 53 |
| Did My Mother Have Affairs While She Was Married? | 54 |
| My Sister Returns from a Year Away at Boarding School | 55 |
| Winning Hand | 57 |
| I Lost My Lost My Baby Teeth and My Virginity in a House Eaten by Termites | 58 |
| The Committee | 59 |
| Trying to Pick Out a Father's Day Card for You | 60 |
| What's Left Unsaid | 61 |

| | |
|---|---|
| A Short Treatise on Manners and Good Breeding | 62 |
| Recipe for Success | 63 |
| After Being Together for Forty Years | 64 |
| The Hoarding Game | 65 |
| A Life Cut Short | 67 |
| Late Lunch at Luigi's | 69 |
| 1968 Yearbook | 70 |
| Hearing Is the Last to Go | 71 |
| Omen | 72 |

## IF I WERE TO DIE TOMORROW

| | |
|---|---|
| Dandelion of Plymouth Rock | 79 |
| The Jade Plant | 80 |
| This Extra Fat | 81 |
| At the Consignment Shop | 82 |
| A Day Out on the Town Before Our Wedding Tomorrow | 83 |
| Cross Your Heart | 84 |
| What I Want | 85 |
| Ode to Be a Twin | 86 |
| That Shaft of Light | 87 |
| White Curtains | 88 |

| | |
|---|---|
| If I Were to Die Tomorrow | 89 |
| A Good Night for a Seven-Year-Old Boy | 90 |
| Headed North | 91 |
| He Was Only 46 | 92 |
| The Bed in My Head Room | 93 |
| Daybreak | 94 |
| Reliquary for a Best Friend | 95 |
| What Was It About Summer Camp | 96 |
| Vestigial Flock | 97 |
| The Inchworm | 98 |
| Head Count | 99 |
| Once Upon a Time | 100 |
| When I Come Back | 101 |
| | |
| Notes | 102 |
| Acknowledgements | 103 |
| Dedications | 104 |
| About the Author | 105 |

*for Laure-Anne*

# EPISTLES TO GOD

I know You already know that
You know me better than that.

# (PARENTHESES)

Pressing through the passageway, we come—
come into the light, take our first breath.

Pulling back the cowl, we see
our parentheses open (

We've come from that place to this.
Now we forget—what place was that?

Growing busy, we go from one place to the next
until we find ourselves in that place again—

the one we recall
we've longed for all along.

Leave fear at the door, shrug off the shroud,
move through this secret passageway,

release your last breath—
$\qquad\qquad\qquad$ Go .)

# SECOND-BORN DAUGHTERS

Perhaps I am one of those
Chinese daughters:
the second girl born live—only
one child was meant to thrive.

One of those Chinese daughters
whose mouth was tamped
with sand or put up
for adoption in some foreign land.

A daughter
wrapped in blue cloth,
laid down on a corner,
brought home by a stranger,
and suckled on fish broth.

She and I, being
those second born daughters,
those second-hand daughters,
those castoff girls,

perhaps we both speak
that secret language,
the language where a word goes
missing every night,
abandoning its shadow
in the morning light.

# WOMB WITH A VIEW

Those marks—are they my older sister's footprints
where she put her feet up on the wall
to stretch the confines of this sac?

I can sense the salty scent of her still
lacing this liquid I dare not drink.

In the pink light—a rope of fresh-water
pearls swings around me in this sea of bliss

while I swirl in an eddy of muffled songs,
their words working their way to me—

watery sound waves I match to my mother, unseen,
who soon will pull this thumb—

such succor—from my mouth.

# LETTING GO

*It's time to stop sucking that thumb!*

*If you can't do it by yourself, we'll put
a glove on that hand of yours—
I'll tape it closed at the wrist—
or maybe hot pepper would be better.*

My older sister relishes my mother's threats,
joins in the fray, calls me *Baaaaby!*
hunts me down to peck circles around me,
pawk, *Buck, buck, buckteeeth!*

My thumb. Can I ever give it up?
I'm attached to it. It's attached to me.

And there's my younger brother sucking
*his* all the time—first the right, then the left.
Both thumbs, always wet.

I limit my sucking to nighttime now.
To further soothe myself, I burrow
my left index finger into my hair—
knot up the strands, make a mess.

I decide. It's up to me—
make up my mind—*is this it?*
I'm the only one who can do this—
I don't need help—*it's over.*

Tonight, tucked tight in bed,
flat on my back, hands wedged
beneath my thighs, I tell myself,
*Time to give it up.*

And I do.

# WHEN OUR PARENTS GO AWAY, WILLY COMES TO STAY

*Wilhelmina Frederika Legeer, World War II member of the Dutch Resistance.*

A colorless mole holds her steel-
rimmed glasses in place. Five-foot-two
in sturdy shoes, she towers over us—
aged seven, eight and nine.

Our Commandant, we jump as
she barks throughout the day—
her voice so loud, does she think us deaf?

At dinner, she chronicles what the Nazis
did to Jews. We sit rapt,
absorbing new long words
over porcelain plates of peas,
potatoes and grey stewed meat.

*Skin-grafting, vivisection, gas chamber*—
dried, stretched Jewish flesh
lampshades adorned Nazi quarters.
In their labs, past due pregnant women
hung upside down. Legs tied shut.

Willy tells us how The Resistance ran guns,
dug tunnels, and smuggled secret messages
through to the front lines.

Deprivation, *ra/tion/ing*,
she rivets us with stories of hunger—
renders us grateful for our food.

She tells us all this while
our parents are
                gone.

# THE NEW COOK

*Molly Proven—she's so jolly!*
*You're going to love her—*

A heavy-set dimple-cheeked woman
holding out a tray of warm chocolate
cookies—that's what I imagine.

Molly perches on the kitchen chair,
straight back, bone-thin legs crossed,
right foot swinging back and forth.
Two ochre talons pinch a Lucky Strike.

Tufts of hair stand on end above
her bulging forehead—*is that a wig?*
Bug eyes glower at me.

Before her on the table, a cup of instant
coffee, black, and dry white toast—
her steady diet, I will come to learn.

*What's for dinner?* I dare to ask, picturing her
stabbing at a shower curtain with a butcher knife.

She waits a beat, takes a long
pull on her cigarette, exhales
in my direction, then says,
*Tripe and trolley cars.*

# CLAMMING

When the salt and mud stink signaled
low tide—time to dig for clams—
we'd grab pitchforks, pails in hand.

Our house sat on a bluff overlooking
the Long Island Sound. The tidal creek
ebbed at the foot of our hill.

Our sneakers tied nice and tight, we'd run
down the steep trail to the murky strip below.

Aiming sharpened tines at air holes
in the silt, we'd dig and upend buried
little necks, careful not to crack
their tender shells, then haul our spoils
up the hill
        for dinner—fresh steamers,
butter, corn on the cob.

            ***

I think it was May—we were away—
thieves rowed up the creek,
hiked that same steep trail,
entered our house from the back.

They tore pillowcases off our beds,
stuffing them with my parents'
jewelry, family silver and Dad's
collection of gold coins.

And my velvet jewelry box, they stole
that, too, with my gold dog pin—the one
with the turquoise eye Granny gave me,
and a heart-shaped scab—
                    picked off during a summer
                                    thunderstorm.

In the bottom of that case—
fingernail clippings: three short of a complete set
I'd spent a whole year growing out
to send to Revlon, for $100.

***

The police suspected an inside job—
my father *knew* it was my brother's
no-good-rotten friend, who lived
just down the road. He knew
our house inside out.

***

Nothing was ever recovered.

***

In my dreams, I see him—
a shadow in the dark, running
down the hill to the waiting boat below,
weighed down with heavy pillowcases,
making clinking sounds, clattering
as he goes,
happy as a clam
at high tide—

undetected.

# HOW TO BE A THREE-YEAR-OLD

Tear your clothes off the minute you get home.
Wear your underpants on your head.
Try on grown-up shoes and clomp around in them.
Load up your suitcase with toys, drag it across the floor.
Dump it out.
Build a fort out of sofa cushions.
Hide something and then immediately point to it.
Ask someone to read you the same book 100 times.
As your eyelids droop say, *I'm not tired!*
Be reminded not to tease the dog then tease the dog.
Tell Daddy you like Mommy better.
And Mommy you like Daddy better.
Stand on your chair and mush mashed potatoes with your hands.
Say *poopie* when you can't think of anything else to say.
After your first hair cut announce, *That didn't hurt!*

## ABOUT MORONS

A cross between a mole and a mouse,
I thought a moron was a type of rodent—
but walked on two hind legs. I knew

it was *maroon*—the color of a moron's fur—
and wore a belted trench coat, with a slit
in back where its tail stuck out.

I always checked behind the bathroom door—
for that's where I thought morons lived, but
never saw one, although I sometimes heard

skittering about on porcelain, the sound of nails
clicking on the sink as a moron tiptoed past
the medicine cabinet, afraid to wake the sleeping pills.

# TEACUP PAREIDOLIA

Heavy cream meets Earl Grey.

A continent starts to form.

      The earth
keeps shifting.

Giant salamanders                        cross its seas.

The
polar
caps
now
gone.

Foam swirls spiral
                  above—
like a hurricane from

What is not to love about a world
I can swallow in just one sip?

# HUNTING UP A POEM

No more sitting at this desk, chin in palm,
eyes glazed over, staring at the pad,
the wall, nothing at all.

Go outside!
Where all good poems hide
in live oak branches
or loll in those crispy spiked leaves,
home to hungry big-eared rats.

That's where poems stay holed up.

Wait for the wind to wrest them
from their cut-and-pasted paper nests
and scatter them about the yard.

Rake them up—
make them up
into piles—sorting out
the long ones from the short.

Be quick! Before another gust
comes along and blows them all away—

                                       stuff your pockets! Hurry!

# FRITTER THE DAY AWAY

    It starts with intention—just one
    thing I intend to do—

    then it fragments,
    litter scatters
                  as the day blows
    apart into little pieces
    that stick their noses
    into other people's business,
               cause distraction,
                          pull me
    away from all the things
    I was meant to do,
    had planned to do—

    wait. What were they again?

# EPISTLES TO GOD

*1960*

You, bearded man, God—
            in long robes sitting on Your throne in heaven, You have three parts? That doesn't make any sense. You can be a father, *and a son, and* a ghost, all at the same time? *And* that ghost always shows up as a dove. So, You're a bird, too? *And* why did Your son turn His body into bread and His blood into wine—*and* make His disciples eat and drink Him? So, if You can do all that, can you stop my brother and sister from fighting? *And*, can You give us world peace, *and* can You feed all the hungry children?

*1967*

Omniscient God: You see me
everywhere. You are everywhere.
I'm on to You now. I know Your
church. You're just after money.
So is the Pope. Everybody says
he's a *fallacy*.

Because, if You are so good, why
world hunger? Why the wars? Why
saddle me with such an enormous nose,
stringy hair, greasy pimples? You're *cruel*.

Looking in the mirror, I pray daily to die.
On the bus ride home, all the boys call me
*Big Nose... Jew—how did they let you
into the country club, Jew?* What is a Jew
anyway? Why is it a bad thing?

I could care less about the country club.
All I know is I want to fit in.

I tell them, *I broke my nose. How*,
they want to know. *I stepped on it.*
Suddenly, not a peep from
the seats on the bus.

Dear Lord,
      Please spare me. Just let me be
Invisible—like You—so I can hear
what everyone says about me.

2020

How could I have cared that much, God?

My hair's gone white, now.
I've grown to love my nose
and pimples no longer sprout.
My petition to You is:

let me speak all languages and perfectly
play every musical instrument.
How I long to make resonant sounds now,
to be heard, seen and belong.

Oh God, here we are: we've come full circle.

You, still invisible, You, all-seeing—
me, no longer needing to know
what anyone says about me.

      I know You already know that
      You know me better than that.

# THE GLIMPSE

    My dead sister—in my eyes—
    I see her just now in the mirror.
    In my eyes, it isn't her just now,
    it is just a glimpse of her.

    It isn't her making herself known to me.
    It is just a glimpse of her,
    a sparkle,
    making herself known to me—
                             only to me—
    a sparkle, then she is gone.
    Only to me in the mirror—
    then she is
    gone, my dead sister.

# YOU, SLEEPING BESIDE HER

Did it come as a surprise—
that you could fall in love again
after I've been dead for over seven years?
*I'll never marry again*, you said.

That you could fall in love again—
even though you swore,
*I'll never marry again*, you said—
now someone new shares your bed.

Even though you swore—
you, who thought no one could ever take my place—
now someone new shares your bed—
you, sleeping beside her.

You, who thought no one could ever take my place—
another woman has done just that.
You, sleeping beside her,
you let a new wife take my place.

Another woman has done just that.
After I've been dead for over seven years,
you let a new wife take my place.
Did it come as a surprise?

# ACCIDENTS HAPPEN

Her latest accessories? Plaster casts and cloth
ace bandages—their stretchy ends joined by metal hooks.
*I tripped over the cat*, she says.
The next day it could be *fell, bringing in wood*.
There's always some excuse.

We know all about the "accidents," so frequent now,
the puffy face, how those droopy eyes signal us
that the bottle has drawn her—
into its green glass goblet world
of blurry vision, slurry speech, wobbly steps.

The upstairs neighbor man finds her, shudders
he'll never get over seeing her—three days dead,
bloated, spread-eagle on the floor, mouth agape,
nightgown torqued above her waist.

Three days now the cats have gone
unfed. Flies fester
on the windowsill. My God! The stench!

*Let me write the obituary*, I suggest.

Her only blood relative shakes his head, *No,
not worth the ink.*

# QUID PRO CROW

For forty days I've fed them now—
this family of crows.

At dusk, their taffeta rustle
alerts me—they're flying in
to peck and pick at the evening.

Chopped cubes of stale white
bread, last night's chicken
carcass torn apart—how
they like the fatty skin!

When will they bring me something in return?

I wait here for a token—
some shiny piece of foil, an acorn or a ring—
only a black feather
dropped nearby, where I sit.

Is this the gift I've been waiting for
all along? A quill—with which to write?

# MY SISTER'S RING

It's just the two of us in the funeral home foyer—
my dead sister's husband Paul and me.

Here comes the mortician, trudging up
from the basement where my sister's body lies.

Out of breath, she puffs, *What a bear that was!*
*Had to cut her finger off. Needed tinsnips.*

*Here*—she drops the sapphire band
into Paul's outstretched hand—

he picks it from his palm. *Here*—he says—
*your sister's ring, don't you want it now?*

I gasp, clasp my hands behind my back.

What ever happened to using liquid soap?
Was there no other way?
Where's her finger now?

My thoughts sneak down
those basement stairs, peek through
that filmy window of the swinging door,
see her body, nude on a steel gurney,
hands folded across her chest.

And there, tucked in her frozen grip,
like a pencil, is her finger—
that middle one she so loved
to give me—I give mine
back to her—my final salute.

*Don't you want your sister's ring?*
*Don't you want your sister's ring?* Paul repeats.

*No, thank you*, I say.

# THE ALTAR

    I do
    you do
    he/she does
    we do
    you (pl) do
    they do

    Why does everyone *do*
    except *he* and *she*, who only *do*
    when they come together—
    when they become *they*,
    only then do they *do*?

# THE EXTRAORDINARY SEX LIFE
# OF THE SLIPPER LIMPET

Did you know—

slipper limpets are sequential
hermaphrodites? They can change
from male to female or female to male.

In their female stage, they flaunt
their kitten-heeled mules with marabou trim

and when they want to parade their maleness,
they change into sporty slip-on scuffs.

On those hazy in-between days—
the slipper limpet most often
opts for flip flops.

# AT THE PIER

    She watches from the rear
    the handsome man—tanned back—
    as he two-finger flicks a hot half-
    smoked cigarette onto the wooden pier.

    She fears he could start a fire,
    and he does, in her.

    Below her, high tide finishes
    pounding—teasing the shore—
          in and out, harder and faster—
                    white foam forming.

    She turns back—sees that still-lit butt—lying
    there on the old pier, smoldering.

    This time
    she steps on it.

# INSIDE OUT

You lie between the rhythm of his breath
and the lapping of the sea.

Foam pillow inside—sea foam out.
Unlit inside—full moon out.

Tossing, turning, sheets inside out,
you bring the outside in.

Your breath, which cadence will you choose?

The gasps of the snores by your ear?
The crash of the waves on the shore?

Or will you pull yourself from both these sides,
these tides, and breathe alone, on your own?

# SETTLING THE ESTATE

The dust has settled,
so have the ashes.

There is still something
left to settle—the score.

I LOST MY BABY TEETH
AND MY VIRGINITY
IN A HOUSE EATEN BY TERMITES

They taught me over time how all things
eventually come apart.

# WHY

does my mother make me
wear an undershirt? Make me
bundle up? It's 90° outside!

Why?

I'm sweating like a pig.
How could she not know—
it's stupid to wear two shirts?

*Why?*

I ask. I ask. I ask.

*Why?*

She doesn't answer, busies
herself in her top drawer,
won't look me in the eye.

*Why?*

Finally—she blurts out, *Nipples!*

# MONDRIAN'S SOCK DRAWER

Mondrian filled his drawers
with black grids
of primary-colored
cashmere socks
and white
fly-flapped underwear.

Gazing at this closet utopia,
he limited his formal vocabulary
to *ahhh*.

# RED

1958

We share the bathroom, my sister and I—
draw a Maginot line dividing it in half.
She gets the sink and bathtub faucets.
I get the toilet and back of the tub.

*I can do everything in the toilet*, I brag.

After dinner, we take a bath—
she in front—me in back.
The skin on her upper arm looks
moist and tender. I take a bite,
clamp down hard.

Her shrieks surprise me—
*How could that hurt?* I wonder,
as the mark I made on her reddens.

1966

My sister sits on the bathroom floor
using her new electric razor. Its yellow
beam lights the way for whirring blades.

She looks up at me in my Madras shorts—
eyes my furry shins. *Wolfman*—she says—
*It's time to shave your legs.*

*Can I try your Lady Sunbeam?* I beg.

*NO!* She snaps, unplugs it from the wall. Holds it—
her trophy—above her head, struts back to her room,
kicks the door shut—locks me out.

In the medicine chest, I find her old razor.
Here's the shaving foam—whipped cream
with a grown-up smell. I want to lick it.
I spread it on my leg and aim the razor.

*Should I go with the grain?* I ask
her bolted door. Silence shuts me up.

I decide to go with the grain.

Stroking the blade firmly down my calf,
I plow a pink path, nick my ankle bone.
Red courses down my foot. I feel no pain.

*Does this mean I'm a grown-up now?*

# THE NEIGHBORS' TOMMYROT

This fine-feathered cox-combed flapper-
doodle will be the end of me if he throws
his crow into our yard one. more. time.

That rooster drives me crazy—drives me
to Google to seek a solution for its cock-a-
doodle-doo that echoes off our walls.

Is there a recipe to make this sack of
codswallop into soup before he struts
his nuts into our yard one. more. time?

Ah! Here's the remedy:

*Catch that cock—succor
to none—shove him in a box.
Tape the lid down tight.*

*Load him in your car and drive
him North, down a tree-lined lane.*

*Where the thickets are thickest,
shove the box between two rocks,
unseal the lid and let him go.*

Let him go.

# TO THE WEALTHY OLD MAN WHO LEFT HIS WIFE OF FIFTY YEARS FOR A MUCH YOUNGER WOMAN

*How could I be so lucky?* Is that
what you ask yourself as you feast
your eyes on your new young wife
stepping from the shower after hours
of making love to you?

She baits you with her bought breasts.
Can you resist them? Why not
regress back into your mother's arms—
suckle at her breasts again?

But these fresh teats give no milk.
They are a lure, turgid like your pants-
dwelling homunculus, who's so cocksure
you're alive again.

Desire swells—revived again,
you live to smell the roses
tattooed on her smooth inner thigh—

you're high on life—happy to stay
awake all night in this juicy new world,
keeping death at bay.

And what of your shucked-off wrinkled old
wife? Left to consider her options—
she wonders, should she get a cat?

# MARRIAGE METAPHORS

Monogrammed wedding present—
a set of blue terry towels.

*Why my maiden name initials?* I ask
my aunt—twice-married.
Her reply, *Trust me—your towels*
*will long outlive your marriage.*

The first ten years of wedded bliss,
those towels, thick and thirsty,
lick the moisture from taut breasts
and backs, swaddle children after baths.

At twenty years of married life,
they fade to dingy grey. Their edges
fray where the cat has snagged
its claws. They sop up rains
that breach the windows left

                            open

by mistake.

After thirty year of knotted ties,
things change for them—

                    tired infidels—

turned into tatters,
torn into squares—
rags, they lie lifeless
in a pile under the sink.

After forty years, those terry shreds
fall apart, limp their way to the trash.

What made me keep them for so long?
Maybe to prove to my aunt—
she was wrong.

## LYING IN THE CONFESSIONAL

I line up sins inside my head—
a row of baby ducks—waiting to go
inside the confessional:

*Bless me, Father, for I have sinned.*
*It has been one week since my last confession.*
*I accuse myself of disobeying*
*my parents X times, fighting*
*with my brother and sister X times,*
*and lying X times.*

*Now for all the sins I cannot*
*remember, I am truly sorry.*

I only see the priest's shadow,
making the sign of the cross as I lie—
confess to things I've rarely done—
I change the number every week.

The priest gives me my penance:
Ten *Hail Marys* and three *Our Fathers*—
or is it the other way around?

It doesn't matter. I must atone
for things I've seldom done.

Head bowed, I kneel—get to work polishing
the golden beads on my rosary—a first
communion gift from my godfather,
whom I hardly ever see, but who sent me
a rabbit fur bonnet for Christmas last year.

# MAYBE YOU KNOW THAT GUY—

the one who brags about
all the women he slept with?

Goes into every detail in
long poems—four pages long—

bores you until he admits he's
sad—the woman he loved

most left him. I've been left, too.

No finger can plug the hole
in the dyke. That loss keeps

seeping out. It leaches
the sunset—drains the twilight black—

twists the night's wet sheets.
Maybe that's when it dawns on me—

he and I—we are more alike than not.

# DID MY MOTHER HAVE AFFAIRS WHILE SHE WAS MARRIED?

Did she do it with Anton Ivanov, the arborist
with Popeye arms? At first, he came for the trees
and then he came for her—to give her "Russian lessons."

*** 

What about Brother Joseph, the Benedictine monk?
She did buy *all* his Gregorian music. He did come
for dinner *all* the time, then left the Priory
and married someone else.

***

Or Stan Mosler, that red-haired Jimmy Durante
look-alike artist? She commissioned him to do ten
paintings, and invited him salmon fishing with us
in Canada, where he wore that olive-green Speedo.

***

Ralphie the stable boy? I wonder—did his wife drive
into the river to kill herself because my mother was having
an affair with her husband?

***

Then there was Dr. Payne, the chain-smoking chiropractor
with the nicotine-stained beard. He stuck his finger in
every orifice to do his *adjustments.*

***

On second thought, maybe it's just as well I never knew.

# MY SISTER RETURNS FROM A YEAR AWAY AT BOARDING SCHOOL

It was a glamorous affair to travel by air
in the 60's. Skirts cut just above the knee,
pill box hats, white gloves, the stewardesses
handed out cigarettes for free.

We're picking my sister up from the airport.
I steal a satin pointy bra
from my mother's drawer—stuff
the cups with rolled-up coarse wool socks.

I stretch on a white poor boy
ribbed shirt, tight as can be,
over a floral wrap skirt. Watermelon
Pappagallos, John Lennon sunglasses—set to go!

On the expressway, my mother takes her eyes
off the road, lands them on my chest. *Oh my!*
*You've inherited Granny's boobs.*

I glow, happy she notices my new shape—
then blush. *How long can I keep this front up?*

We park. Arrive just in time.
From a distance—that slight slump—
it's her. I'm excited. My chest
itches, each scratchy ball starts to shift.
I rearrange as she comes closer.

My heart sinks. This can't be her.
*That outfit!* Dirndl skirt, unbuttoned
shirt, two-inch Gucci heels!

*That makeup!* Those racoon eyes,
rimmed with kohl, mascara troweled on
so thick—those parakeet-blue-shadowed lids
flick open and closed below tweezed brows.

*Hi*, she breathes out Listerine.
Full lips shimmer a deep pink pout.
Then another stink wafts my way—
an overlay of Jean Naté.

*What a slut*, I think—
adjust my shifting chest,
snug my shirt down tight.
Nice and tight.

# WINNING HAND

From Palm Beach toy store to rodent-ridden
A-frame in Vermont, our Barbies get around.

Granny buys them for my sister and me:
she, the brunette, me—I get the blonde. Both
wear black and white bathing suits and red cork heels.
I like their earrings—pins you push into their heads.

New England summer days when we aren't picking
rocks from the field, and Mary comes to play, we bring
a pack of cards and our dolls, loaded in their wardrobe
cases, down to the farmhand's vacant quarters, climb
the ladder to the second floor, set up shop in the hot
stale air and deal the cards on the rough pine deck.

Flies smack their heads against the window, so filthy
we can't see out. I choose my winning hand—
The Friday Night Date set—rack up early points with two
orange drink glasses, black plastic tray. It takes four
more rounds to be robbed of earrings and the shoes.

Counting the white chemise, and light blue felt
jumper, red birdhouse glued onto its skirt—I tally nine
advantages to beat the odds and win
Barbie Strip Poker.

# I LOST MY LOST MY BABY TEETH AND MY VIRGINITY IN A HOUSE EATEN BY TERMITES

It took millions of tiny mouthfuls
to raze it to the ground. Industrious
workers, they chewed our home
right to the bone, leaving heaps
of sawdust—rust-colored confetti—
strewn about the yard.

They taught me over time how all things
eventually come apart.

Take my mouthful of baby teeth—
six years for their roots to disintegrate
as adult teeth erupted beneath,
pushed their way through.

Take my virginity—at seventeen
I asked for that. It didn't take long
that night in an upstairs room—
that summer heat wrapping
the two of us into one.

When we unfurled, something came
apart in me. I started to delaminate—
come apart at the seams—
I told no one.

*Could it happen to me?* I ticked
my days—petrified—missed a month,
sick with worry—I'd be responsible
for a little beating heart. Then

my blood began to flow—relief.
I shifted my belief that somehow,
I was above it all.

# THE COMMITTEE

Yet another meeting—the tenth so far this week.
Exhausted from the note taking,
my pencil takes a break—
doodles in the margins.

The committee Chair? *Eggplant* without a doubt.
Smooth and lustrous—the perfect diplomat.

Next to her, I outline *Fiddlehead Fern*,
the thin-lipped accountant with the constant frown.

And Dhyan, the lump
of porridge? Never says a word?
I sketch her as *Cauliflower*.

Across the table, that member
rough around the edges—
well, *Kale* comes to mind.

My pencil strokes need to widen
to capture *Onion*, our stout Co-chair
who peels back all the reasons why
some things just can't be done.

And now it's my turn, as Secretary,
I should get to pick—

I draw *Belladonna* for myself—
the deadly nightshade.

If looks could kill, I would.

# TRYING TO PICK OUT A FATHER'S DAY CARD FOR YOU

I scan this rack's selection,
looking for the perfect fit—hmmm,

you aren't the golfing Dad, always on the course,
the lazy-ass-swinging-in-a-hammock Dad, no,
neither are you that Dad out at the Bar-b-que,
beer can in your hand.

Why are Dads always sitting
in rowboats fishing
or in recliners, remotes glued fast to their fists?

After a half-crank turn of the display,
I sink into the same ennui of all the cards
I see—you're not the neck-tied Dad
rushing off to work, nor
king-of-the-castle jerk
padding around the house,
plastic slippers, open robe.

No, after a visit to this whiny turnstile
full of tributary cards,
I come away with just one notion—
you are not the run-of-the-mill

farting,
belching,
lazy son-of-a-bitch,
gluttonous,
dead drunk,
zoned out,
never present,
self-absorbed
miscreant Dad that Hallmark makes you out to be.

# WHAT'S LEFT UNSAID

Our dog Dutchman dresses just like me
in every family Christmas card—candy
cane pajamas, flannel nightcap, pompom!
And on each furry paw, non-skid-slippers.

On his birthday every year, he wears
a silly hat and sits next to me, waiting
for his cake—a dogfood-filled Pyrex plate,
wreathed with wet Milk Bone biscuits.
He always lets me blow his candles out.

Strange—the day he isn't here
to greet me after school—

*Where's Dutchman?*

My mother can't say
he's dead.

I understand now.
It was hard for her to talk
about the death of her favorite
child. I loved him too.

# A SHORT TREATISE ON MANNERS AND GOOD BREEDING

*A little ship went out to sea,*
                         *to bring the soup back to me.*

*That's* the polite way to eat your soup—
it's best to push your spoon
away from you as you fill it up.

Elbows *off* the table,
           (we know, we know,)
                  this is *not* a horse's stable.

If you make that grumpy face—
beware—it may just freeze in place.

Posture—*posture*—POSTURE—
or your slump will become a hump.

You are *not* a mason troweling mortar on a brick,
so butter your bread on the plate.

It's *curtains*, not *drapes*, *sofa*, not *couch*, *rug* not *carpet*.

Above all, don't forget to curtsy and say *thank you.*
And smile! *What do you have to complain about?*

# RECIPE FOR SUCCESS

    Follow up.
           Follow up.
                    Follow up.

# AFTER BEING TOGETHER FOR FORTY YEARS

Are you my affliction or am I my own? After all,
aren't we all part of one another?

The things I dislike in you so much a part of me?
And vice versa, of course.

In a tsunami, you would have grabbed onto a tree,
floated to safety. I'd have gone down under. Gladly.

Not drowning in some old folks' home
having someone else wipe for me,

I would have been:
A hero!
     Young...
            Vibrant!
                  In her prime!
What a waste!

You'd have loved young women
bringing casseroles to our house.

# THE HOARDING GAME

A narrow trail leads to the chair
    where you sit in your 10 x 12 room
        at the assisted living center.

I smell a hint of bonito fish flakes
    mixed with lanolin and a splash of
        turtle terrarium.

You assure me above the drone
    of the oxygen concentrator,
        *There will be no parting with any of it.*

No—not planning to part with—the giant stuffed bear
    (topped off with a Dolly Parton wig)
        (holding a pink plastic microphone)
            (commanding a spot on the prow of your bed)

    the raft of brand-new L.L Bean sweatshirts
        (wrong size—wrong color, their price tags a-blow)
            (bobbing in the back of the room)

    (in the breeze of the air conditioning unit)
        (that cooling tower on wheels with dryer vent duct work)
            (snaking towards a hole in the window)

    (where only a little daylight can squeeze into the room)
        (through the smallest cracks in the montage's pattern)
            (of top-less mermaid and dancing starfish)

    (gel stickers that crowd the picture window's starboard)
        (an offshoot of the Great Pacific Garbage Patch)
            (swirling here on glass in landlocked Vermont)

No—not planning to part with your library
    (of three waist-high stacks of unread)
        (paperback whodunnits that will run)
            (out of time before their mysteries are solved)

or the boxes of anime and X-rated tapes
    (your brother sent and you plan to watch)
    (even though you have no VCR)

*There must be something that can go*, I say.
    My eyes land on waterspouts of Styrofoam—
        funnels filled with varied levels of brown

syrupy liquid—sweet tea from McDonald's—
    the only thing, you say, that quells your thirst.
        Forty of these cups—flotsam in this sea of stuff—

I hold one up.

    *How many do you need?* I ask.
    *Seven*, you say.
    *May I?* I ask.
    *Yes*, you say. *Please do.*

# A LIFE CUT SHORT

I got the news
this morning.
My brother-in-law died
last night.

I call his wife.
*I'm so sorry,* I say.
She has people there,
so I keep it short.

I call his brother,
who says,
*I called my brother
every day
before he died,
just to check in on him.*

Now his nephew
is on the other line—
so, I cut it short.

I call his sister.
No answer—
I tell the silence—
*I'm so sad, so sorry.*

She calls right back.

*I'm going to go
to the nurses' station
to let them have it.*
Her Irish blood boils.
*Blacken all their eyes.
He shouldn't have died.*

*Too soon.*
*They sent him*
*home too soon.*

She needs to call
her daughters.
I make it short.

I call my husband's office.
He's busy now.

*Your brother is dead.*

He's too busy to talk right now.
He needs to keep it short.

I hang up, say,
*I'm so sorry.*

# LATE LUNCH AT LUIGI'S

*I am still working*, I say
to the waiter who tries to take my plate—
I am working.

I didn't grow the spinach, bake the bread
or milk the cow to make the butter.
I didn't lay the cloth, set the table, pour the water.

I just sit there and eat.
And I'm not finished yet.

# 1968 YEARBOOK

A long-lost friend comes.
It's been more than 40 years.

I pull out our grade school yearbook.

How clearly I remember being
captain of the hockey team,
class president and the lead
in the operetta!

*Want to take a look?* I ask.
*Yes, let's!* she says.

There! Her large loopy writing
takes up the whole front plate.
Her name autographs most every page.
We were, after all, best friends back then.

But—where are the photos of our younger selves?

I search for myself in
the student council lineup,
the hockey team montage,
the operetta's candid shots.

How odd!
My friend is not
in any of those either.

# HEARING IS THE LAST TO GO

If that's true, then what would be the last words or sound I would want to hear?

I know it would not be

a

  leaf

    blow

      er

   .

# OMEN

    A crow flies above
    From the sky a black feather
    Morning's business card

# IF I WERE TO DIE TOMORROW

I'm scared of going bald.

# DANDELION OF PLYMOUTH ROCK

We came over together
on the Mayflower

the dandelion and I.

Kindred spirits,
both blonde,

now blanching,
full-sphere white crowns—

that ride the wind
instead of the waves,

our hair-like parachutes
in search of a moss-covered rock
on which to land.

# THE JADE PLANT

It started out small when you left.
I watched it grow like you.

I'd wash its chubby leaves
the same way I'd wash your little hands.

Water it, then ignore it, intermittently.
Did I do the same to you?

# THIS EXTRA FAT

It's like another person
is sitting on my lap.

# AT THE CONSIGNMENT SHOP

Why are the clothes I drop off
    the very ones my eyes pick out,
        my hands land on—the ones I want to buy—
            when I come back to shop a week later?

# A DAY OUT ON THE TOWN
# BEFORE OUR WEDDING TOMORROW

A two-legged dog greets us at
the entrance to the Katmandu Zoo.

Only back legs, none up front,
it hops towards us like a kangaroo—
undulating past the legless beggar
who, moving towards us, slides himself
along on a piece of cardboard,
pulling his torso down the street
with a rusty handled iron in each hand.

How I believed back then that
two lives came together to make one.

# CROSS YOUR HEART

Does he know I have my fingers crossed
this wedding day under my bouquet?

And when I say *I do*, does he know
I cross my toes inside my shoes, too?

My white silk sleeves hide the rip
tide pulling me out to sea—pulling me

down, trying to drown me as the band
plays the only song they know—

*Never on Sunday*—does he know that tune
is about the small-town prostitute who

did it every day but took her Sundays off?
Is he as scared as I am?

Cross your heart, hope to die,
tell me—is this all just one big lie?

# WHAT I WANT

Dear Santa,
     This year, for my tenth birthday—my parents were away—left my present with the babysitter. Guess what it was. A pen. A gold one—from Tiffany's, engraved with my initials, so I knew it was no mistake. Don't they know me? I'm ten. I'm ten—old enough to know you don't exist—let alone read minds—that doesn't stop me from hoping you'll bring me something really special this year. I don't know what I want. No, wait—I *do* know what I want! I want *you* to figure out what I want.

               ***

The big day is here. It's early—
bathrobe and slippers, brother and sister
                              and me.
We fly to the tree.

There's the steam engine for my brother.
And in its brand-new case, my sister's new guitar.
Everything else is wrapped except—
wait—what's that leather briefcase
doing there? With *my* initials on it?
Oh! I get it—the surprise is *inside*.

Quick! I click the two clasps open,
lift the lid. A gust of fresh new leather—
I breathe it in, hold my breath,
look inside. It's

                                   empty.

## ODE TO BE A TWIN

Matching bowl cuts, matching outfits—
we were *almost* twins.

We were the same height—
while I looked up to you,

you looked down on me—
wanted nothing much to do with me.

If I were your twin,
think of all the attention I would get!

People would jumble our names,
bumble to tell us apart.

I would be the cute one,
you could be the smarty pants.

We'd have our secret language—
eye rolls, lip curls, hand signals.

We'd marry twin brothers whose names,
just like ours, started with an S—

Seth, Sam, Simon, Steven—
I'd call first dibs.

But maybe this isn't what
I've been dreaming of—

getting double attention,
double love—

maybe what needs to happen is
for one of us to leave

this nest of family confusion.
Maybe that one is me.

# THAT SHAFT OF LIGHT

    Water turned into wine.
    Bread loaves made into fish.
    People raised up from the dead.

    Dangling my feet from a wooden pew
    in this cavernous church where amber
    beams pour through Jell-O-colored panes
    of leaded stained-glass,
        I wonder—

        maybe, if I sit in just the right spot,
        let that shaft of light hit me just right—
        *God, see me, perform a miracle just for me.*

# WHITE CURTAINS

She's still alive a year beyond
what all the doctors gave her—
a prize! it is—
           the gift of time.

*How slowly it passes.*

My sister's barren scalp,
land of hairy tufts,
a fairy ring around that hole
they quarried to dig out a potato-
sized tumor from her brain.

Her newfound husband cannot
fathom this looming loss,
cannot let her go.

*She's dying way too fast.*

He paints her toenails red—
as if there's nothing wrong—
blows on them to dry.

Months and months, she rests in bed,
sips small breaths of air—
nectar to the nearly dead.

I lie beside her—my right arm
cramps—I don't dare move.

Above her dragging rales I hear
white curtains flutter in the breeze—
angel wings.

## If I Were to Die Tomorrow,

what would you want to know about me now?
I'm scared of going bald.

I try my best to be a mother. Did I do any better
than my own mother? I yodel at weddings
and knit sweaters for newborns to welcome them.

I play with words, scissors, knives, and matches—
do crossword puzzles in ink with my left hand:
it sounds like I like to brag. I do. Sometimes, I do.

That I am cautious—operating most days
under *condition orange*—preferring to travel
in my head rather than the outside world.

I have trouble minding my own business—
someone else's story can so easily drag me
into the woods.

There are times when I feel great pleasure in being
a victim—let that broken record of *somebody done
somebody wrong* song spin inside my head.

The smells that wake me in the middle of the night,
I wonder: are they signs from departed ones?
Last night it was paprika—Hilda?

Is it loyalty or inertia that makes me stay
in some relationships way too long?
Or is it the devil I know...?

I see humor in even the worst situations.
Know this: it has saved me from myself.
Maybe.

# A GOOD NIGHT FOR A SEVEN-YEAR-OLD BOY

He says *good night* to his parents
        and their drunken friends—
                goes up to bed.

He hears their tires
        crunch the gravel driveway.
                They've all gone out—

he creeps back down.
        It's the ashtrays
                he's after to harvest butts.

Several still have some life left—
        he stows them in a cocktail
                napkin—stuffs it in his robe.

Lining up his lips to the red
        lipstick marks on the glasses,
                he drains the drinks

                and, plucking
        a fat sausage from a platter,
patters back upstairs again.

# HEADED NORTH

       Fred passed away this week.
            My friend. I loved him.
                  In my dream, he flies by
                            as a Canadian goose—
    circles around me once and says,
   *A goose never roosts in a tree—*
then heads North. Alone.

# HE WAS ONLY 46

The day before he dropped dead,
he was here—her brother. He helped
her vacuum and dust.

*It was his heart*, the coroner said.

She came in this morning to iron. How could she
not be thinking of him as she smoothed
the wrinkles from our sheets?

That iron sits cold now, its cord
a twisted, kinked-up, knotted mess.

I take it gently in both hands, work
to uncurl it—milk it—wring
out every last drop of sorrow—
make it lie flat.

# THE BED IN MY HEAD ROOM

A bedroom—painted pale pink. White
linen curtains scrim open windows.

A four-poster bed moors to a buoy
on the briny blue rug.

I tug the goose down duvet—silk, creamy
over my skin—throw back the covers,

four-sheets to the wind—drunk—waiting for you.

# DAYBREAK

The crow's caw cracks
open morning.

Don't wake me yet.

A motorcycle's roar shifts
gears between stop signs.

What's the rush?

I listen. A train whistles,
shrill, in the distant hollow.

The clock can read—7 AM—
somewhere in this world.

Now that somewhere is here,
where I lie—watching dust motes

slowly snow—in that slit
of light slipping in.

# RELIQUARY FOR A BEST FRIEND

I keep you in my phone,
in my contacts list.

On your birthday each year,
my phone reminds me:

your name over a present icon,
white box, red bow.

Every day, I see your face
in my photo scroll.

You're in there. Smiling,
*should I let my hair go gray?*

Yes! Yes! I say.
I want to grow old with you.

But, no—
no—

## What Was It About Summer Camp

that made me want to pack in April?
That made me ready to go
long before it was time to be away
for two months
in the New Hampshire woods?

Was it the slam of screen doors
echoing across the lake? The aluminum
pitchers filled with bright red bug juice?
The soft white bread, smeared
with butter and sugar?

Maybe it was the smell of frogs
in the inch of murk at the water's edge?
Or the overnight canoe trips,
sleeping under Orion?
Was it none of these—

was it because I had found my tribe,
uncovered that part of me
missing at home?
I was noticed—at last.

# VESTIGIAL FLOCK

In the top branches, the last
leaves roost.

Winter wind wants
to shake them loose.

They refuse to head south.

# THE INCHWORM

Hanging by a thread
    that's how I find you.

You light upon my shoulder.
    I will carry you farther
than you've ever been before.
    I will take you up a trail

lined with bougainvillea.
    Your eyes will not see

the beauty spread before us ——
    they will only sense
light and dark. You will turn into a moth.

Attracted by the light, in the dark
    you will fly into a flame

and bring with you no memory
of what you are now:

a small green stripe, stretching out
    to become a full inch

in the immeasurable world
    that lies —— vast
        beyond my shoulder.

# HEAD COUNT

When it gets to be too much,
I count—as I walk—I count
the steps inside my head—
I count—
let those numbers fill
my head—no thoughts—
just numbers in that space.
They push those thoughts out
to a pasture far away
where lay the sheep
I learned to count to fall asleep.

## Once Upon a Time

    there was a
    giant
    princess
    witch
    fairy
    ogre
    wood cutter
    toy soldier

    who lived
    in a castle
    in the trunk of a tree
    in a house in the woods
    under a bridge
    in a cave
    in a match box
    on a cloud.

    Every day, he/she/they would
    sit and weep
    cast spells
    flit about
    say *Fe Fi Fo Fum*
    march around in circles
    chop wood
    eat candy

    until there was nothing left.
    Nothing.

# WHEN I COME BACK

Remember when you were a baby,
sucking your thumb in your crib?

You had no frame of reference,
no sense of time.

Remember when nothing mattered?
Those shadows dancing around the room?

That warm welling up, swaddling your bottom—
its faint familiar smell?

Remember lying there, trying to mouth
what your first word would be?

In my next life, I'm coming back as a baby.

## NOTES

Please do not read every poem literally. I may have taken some poetic license and it is possible that I might have lied a little here and there, and even cheated a bit, particularly on page 57.

No animals were harmed in the making of this book. I did *not* let a rooster named Tommyrot out of a box at the end of a dirt road.

The observant eye may notice that the dashes in "The Inchworm" (page 98) are longer than in any other poem. There may be a measure of truth here.

As far as I know, "tripe and trolley cars" are not a Scottish dish. Why Molly always had them on the dinner menu is beyond me.

If you're wondering what *pareidolia* is, see if you can find an elephant riding a bicycle in the clouds.

Nota Bene: If a heavily buttered slice of Wonder Bread ladened with sugar happily lands on the plate in front of you, to derive significantly enhanced health benefits (or so I've been told), roll it into a ball and take a bite out of it, like an apple.

# ACKNOWLEDGEMENTS

To my husband, Ted, who always says, *Yes!* in answer to: *Want to hear a new poem?* Such love and support sustain me.

To my son, "Adirondack Red" Read Cronin, for making me split my sides with his woodsman impressions and to my son, Wright Cronin, for his insights into and joy of a shared passion, poetry.

My sister, Sandra Read, deserves special mention here and gratitude for always being a little older than me and always one step ahead. I miss you. You live on in many of these poems.

I am indebted to the anthology *While You Wait: A Collection by Santa Barbara County Poets* and *Santa Barbara Literary Journal* for publishing my poems.

If you did not personally appear on any of these pages, I am sorry for the omission. I think of you often and am so pleased you are in my life.

# DEDICATIONS

"How to Be a Three-Year-Old" is for Misha Bean Cronin.

"When I Come Back" is for Saffron Dove Cronin.

"The Inchworm" is for Teddy Lilly Cronin and Saeja Rae Cossart.

"The Extraordinary Sex Life of the Slipper Limpet" is for Karin Muller.

"Mondrian's Sock Drawer" is for Marilee Zdenek.

"The Bed in My Head Room" is for all my present, former, and future lovers. I await you.

"A Short Treatise on Manners and Good Breeding" is for Laure-Anne Bosselaar, who has me on the floor every time I hear her read it out loud. She has promised to recite this poem at my funeral and I'm going to hold her to it. Laure-Anne has helped me understand what *duende* is and encouraged me to discover places I had dared not go before. She has taught me everything I know about writing poetry, especially to trust you, dear reader. Trust me, this book would not have happened without her.

# ABOUT THE AUTHOR

Susan Read Cronin grew up on the shores of Long Island and in the hills of Vermont. She graduated from The Madeira School and went on to complete a degree in English at Williams College. She was the founder, designer, and mail-order purveyor of *Suzo* costumes for children, and is a photographer, bronze casting sculptor, and poet.

For the past twenty years, she has served on the board of Vermont Studio Center. She is the author of *Bronze Casting in a Nutshell*, and a poetry chapbook, *Notices*. She currently resides in Santa Barbara, California.

www.ingramcontent.com/pod-product-compliance
Lightning Source LLC
Chambersburg PA
CBHW020543080526
44583CB00013B/969